P9-CBB-317

Lemon Meringue Pie at Midnight

Lemon Meringue Pie at Midnight

POEMS BY

Maureen Hand

Maureen Hand

PHOTOS BY

Jane Riley

Jane Riley

Thank you to St. Mary's Roman Catholic Church in Amsterdam, NY for permission to photograph their altar for **DIFFERENT ALTARS** and a portion of a stained glass window for **FAR FROM HOME.**

Thank you to Christine Paris and Kelly Paris for use of their photos.

Thank you to Stephanie Persico for "the pie."

Lemon Meringue Pie at Midnight is a work of fiction.
Names, characters, places and incidents are the products of the author's imagination or are used fictitiously. Any resemblance to actual events, locales, or persons, living or dead, is entirely coincidental.

Copyright © 2013 by Maureen Hand (text) and Jane Riley (photos)
All rights reserved. No part of this book may be used or reproduced in any form, electronic or mechanical, including photocopying, recording, or scanning into any information storage and retrieval system, without written permission from the author except in the case of brief quotation embodied in critical articles and reviews.

Printed in the United States of America

The Troy Book Makers • Troy, New York • thetroybookmakers.com

To order additional copies of this title,
contact your favorite local bookstore,
visit www.tbmbooks.com or amazon.com

ISBN: 978-1-61468-199-1

POEMS ARE JUST STORIES
WITH THE BORING PARTS LEFT OUT.

-W.H. AUDEN

Contents

LEMON MERINGUE PIE AT MIDNIGHT

Maybe I'll bake lemon meringue pie
for the funeral…

The blissful years,
I'll bury beneath the garden
to curl around the roots of orchids
and bloom luminous memories.

The painful years,
I'll place on a flaming pyre
to smolder into opaque teardrops
and twist sadness into ashes.

For the eulogy,
I'll wail with mourning doves
to wake embers of fires past
and waltz with wind in my arms.

…maybe we'll fall in love again
   and eat lemon meringue pie at midnight.

WHERE I COME FROM

I come from an icebox on the back porch
and a white enamel kitchen table
trimmed with black
and bottles of my grandfather's
Ballantine Ale.

I come from a house filled with
silence, secrets, and sorrow.
My mother's shrill "Shhhh"
fills every room.

I come from heartache and hangovers
May altars, mortal sin
Friday's stink of creamed cod
Sunday's taste of body and blood.

Where I come from
 I do penance for impure thoughts,
pen purple prose,
go spelunking with Nancy Drew,
float on pink clouds
pushed by Elvis's guitar.

Where I come from
women get married,
have babies,
obey husbands,
live happily ever after.

THE RED UMBRELLA

When I was a child,
I never knew it was beer
that flavored your corny jokes,
or made it such fun to run with you
in the woods with a red umbrella
looking for snake spit
on yellow and orange wildflowers.
When I was a child,
I loved the tilt of your sailor hat
your Irish jig, the shine of your policeman's badge
the green snake that coiled around your arm
the blue birds above your nipples
the pink and blue pig on your right foot
that matched the veins twisting around your nose.
Dear uncle of mine,
I never knew what drunk meant.
I never understood my mother's scorn.
I just knew your lilting laugh
the twinkle in your eye
your smell of White Owl smoke.
Then time passed, and that snake hung
from your arm like a glob of green clay
waiting to detoxify your body.
I fed you strawberry ice cream, and
you whispered with a wink,
"Get me another cold one
and bring the red umbrella."

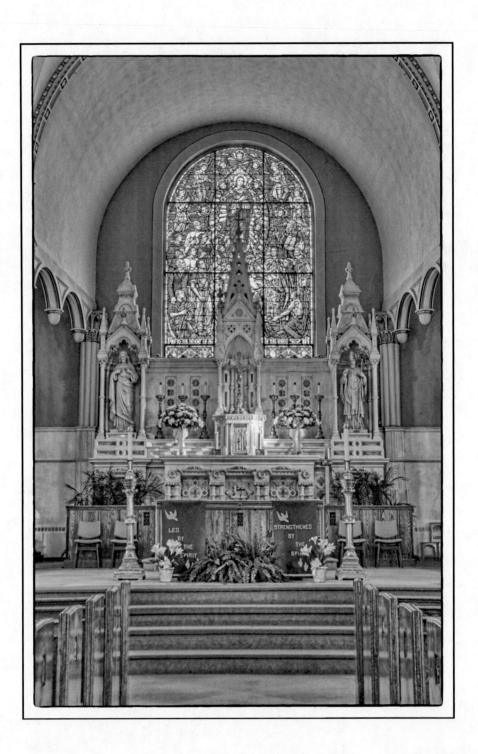

DIFFERENT ALTARS

Angels and saints
embedded in stained glass
peer down on
an altar of white marble statues,
golden candlesticks, and the Tabernacle,
body and blood of Christ—
incense mingles with bells
faithful wait for the Eucharist
Lord I am not worthy
the Word will heal their souls—
My parents worshipped at this altar.

A geometric garden—
round, square, oval
bottles stand like statues,
their intoxicating spirits
tease and trick the mind—
smoke climbs the beveled mirror
loosened tongues chatter aimlessly—
some drink to remember
some to forget, some to
fill the hole in their souls—
My brother worshipped at this altar.

LIQUID LOVER

Tip that glass
let its amber liquid
lick your lips and
tease your tongue
    as you
caress that glass
let its magic potion
intoxicate your mind and
steal your soul
    as you
wallow in that satin wetness
let it soak your veins with venom
destroy your defenses
    as you
slur your mea culpas
savor that sweet elixir
let it make love to you
    before it
leaves you limp
languishing in limbo
locked in eternal emptiness.

SISTER SAYS

The ninth-grade girl's confused...

But if God knows you're going to hell
when you die,
how can you change it, she asks.

You have free will, Sister says.

But if He saw you commit a mortal sin
during His bloody sweat,
how can you not commit it, she asks.

You have free will, Sister says.

But if you're on top of the Empire State Building,
and He knows you're going to jump,
how can you not jump, she asks.

You have free will, Sister says.

How can you have free will
if He already knows
everything you're going to do, she asks.

Don't be a smart aleck.
You have free will.
Pray for the gift of faith, Sister says.

TEEN DREAMS

In my dream, I was the one
who rushed into his open arms,
jumped into his black convertible
ready to chase the magic of the night.
I wanted him to want me.
Him— from the wrong side of the fence
with his tight jeans and black leather jacket.
Please pick me.

In his dream, he wanted her
to dust his lips with kisses
to lie with him in the autumn leaves
and explode like the fourth of July.
Her—one of those easy girls
in short shorts and bright red lips.
He picked her.

My dream ends like a tragic opera
crying my eyes out in loud soprano
Why not me?
as pieces of my broken heart
swirl into the sunset.

His dream ends with him and her
gasping for breath
tangled together like wild grape vines
not connected to time or consequences
caught in the magic of the night.

Over Troubled Water

Yesterday,
 I crawled under this tree lined bridge
of empty branches and withered buds
where the orchard drops into whiteness
and blossoms freeze in the noon-day sun.

Under this bridge, silence pretends
to live happily ever after as it
waits for words that won't speak,
waits for echoes that have no sound.

Like wildflowers, uncertainty grows
under this bridge. Red's bitter aura
taunts the eye like a blood-dimmed tide
flushes a fertile intellect.

Under this bridge is where no lives.
It's where maybe visits.
It's where my eyes drip with you.

IN A WAITING ROOM

I drop off my yellow Bug
its 6,000 mile checkup
oil change, tire rotation
nothing to do but wait

in a waiting room

I hear engines roar
cell phones ring
TV blather
cacophony of being

in a waiting room

I flip pages of **People**
ballooned breasts, painted smiles
who's sleeping with whom
eavesdropping on celebrities

in a waiting room

I scan a newspaper
fire kills family of five
Yankees beat Red Sox
horror and humdrum

in a waiting room

I think about life
time between birth and death
waiting in traffic, in store lines
in doctors' offices

in a waiting room

I remember Godot
the absurdity of it all.
I decide to write about waiting
while I wait

in a waiting room

UNGLUED

The sun's crisp rays crawl through that pane of dust
and dreams and point straight at the glaring glue
stuck on the green and gold wallpapered wall.
I remember when it first unfurled some
years ago, and I thought I could restick
it. With the grace of a gazelle, I climbed
to the top of the ladder. I spread the
glue, caressed the wound, and coaxed, but it would
not adhere, and you announced, "It's too late,"
as glue oozed out like blood, and you just shook
your head. I should have known when it first pulled
away. I should have known it would be hard
to fix. I should have known some rips tear for
a reason. Now, that glitter of glue smirks
like a scar that is no longer bleeding.

A GREEN AND GOLDEN TIME

A green and golden time
at a camp by a lake
brother and sister frolicked
in meadows laced with innocence.
They splashed in ponds and sloshed in mud
squeezed red berries with juice like blood
they skipped the rocks, caught butterflies
flew their kites in the summer skies.
But then, a slimy serpent
slithered through the sunshine
bewitched the boy with devil juice
intoxicated him with bliss.
And so he slipped from halcyon days
into seasons paved with poison—
he hit with deeds—he stabbed with words—
he tripped and fell from grace.
And the years went by without a word
till a stranger found him dead—
he left a trail of broken hearts
and many words unsaid.
A tragic tale of a wasted life
he languished alone in limbo—
the sister cried for the innocence lost,
for the brother who lost his way.

FARM BOY

He's miles away
from cow stink and
yesterday's milk
so warm from the udder,
so sticky on his fingers.

He can't breathe
in a windowless office
in a navy blue blazer
crisp white shirt—buttoned down collar
a choking red tie.

It's hard for plants to root
without barn smells,
manure covered soles, and
rusty tractors
rolling over rows of hay.

FAR FROM HOME

Her scent floats from words tucked in his pocket.
He sits in desert sand and fingers the letter.
That tiny babe in blue beckons to him—

"He's getting big," she says.
"He's going to be blonde—
  looks just like you."

He tastes the smells of home and spits out sand.
He feels her lips, her embrace,
her delicious curves.

"War is hell," they say.
"But what do they know," he sneers,
 embracing the son he has yet to hold.

NEAR THE END

Her love stirs the pudding
swirls it into velvet
creams it so smooth custard
soothes his throat.

She scoops it from the warm pan
dips it into his dish.
His mouth opens like a baby bird's
then closes around the spoon.

Her gentle hand holds the napkin,
puts it to his lips
pats away the pudding
then offers more.

When he is nourished
eyes close.
The end—
so like the beginning.

MISS DICKINSON

Is it presumptuous to ask
About your quest for Truth—
Eternity—the Mystery—
The pen your cherished Sleuth—

You've labored at your writing desk—
No word dropped carelessly—
A verse wrapped-up in Loneliness—
Birthed under Eden's tree—

I too have leafed through lexicons—
No answers to be found—
Life's cryptic message floats above—
Bones buried in the ground—

Your fantasies cavort with Death—
Eve's Original Sin—
Immortality summons you—
The Soul lives free again—

You'll meet Him in the Promised Land—
The Bridegroom holds the key—
Alone at last in Paradise—
Unlock—the Mystery—

Before you leave—do you have time—
Breathe Life into My Words—
Baptize them in the Holy Font—
Renew them with Allure—

I WONDER...

I often wonder Emily—
What do you hide inside—
What stirs the Fodder for your Feasts—
How does the seed decide—

Your Metaphors and Words live on—
Though other stars do fade—
Your blood flows through well-crafted lines
Instead of tiny veins—

But did you ever yearn for Babes—
And not with Words be Blessed—
And did you yearn for Cupid's Shot—
Desires not Confessed—

I Deconstruct your every Word
To glean minutest Signs—
Is this some Sublimation here—
Your images—Sublime—

You stepped right through that firmament—
I hope without regret—
When life beyond the grave began—
I wonder—the Secret—

GRAY AUTUMN MORNINGS

On gray autumn mornings,
one sees the lilac tree
wrinkled and spent
from weight of many seasons.
May's purple brilliance
replaced with fall's faded hue.

On gray autumn mornings,
one readies for winter's shroud.
Pull up impatiens, prune roses,
pluck last of tomatoes,
plant new tulips.
Put everything in order.

On gray autumn mornings,
one fears December's frost.
Will it be harsh?
Will it linger?
Will it burden plants?

On gray autumn mornings,
one's mind flits
from thought to thought
like that bumble bee
hunting for nectar
on the lilac tree's
knotted branches.

CANOEING ON THE KICKAPOO

We're stuck in a sandbar
on the Kickapoo River,
the "crookedest" river in North America,
so they say in Ontario, Wisconsin.

I tell my daughter
it's hard to keep paddling
with all the twists and turns
through marshes and swamps
around rocks and fallen tree trunks.

I tell her it's hard to paddle
and watch muskrats, beavers, waterfowl—
just look in those reeds over there
river royalty eyeing trespassers,
cawing at this red canoe.

Spying on that blue heron is what got us stuck
but sometimes getting stuck is good—
to see wildflowers crane their necks
to feel the sun's blazing rays
or just to squeeze sand in your hand.

COLOR OF A ROSE

In late October
when the burning bush
bleeds the color of a rose
I remember
the magic of long ago Octobers
when we tangled around each other on a
carpet of yellow and orange leaves
you were warm in my veins like a fine wine
you spun your web around me
with lips that promised forever
but
you blew away
like those yellow and orange leaves
and left a heart that bleeds
the color of a rose.

WINTER'S JOURNEY

Pristine snow covers
winter's uncharted trails.
No footprints, no directions
to lead the way—
self-reliance necessary.

Barren branches full of ice
bent like arthritic bones
wait to receive sun's hope
but winter will not waiver—
its grip is strong.

Winter is not for the weak.
Frigid air slows breaths
flakes fall and dim vision
memories of warmer times
rustle within.

Oh, for the gaudy
lime green days of Spring
when cares were few
and desires grew like
sultry nights of summer.

ETHEL'S ROCKING CHAIR

The rich brown arms and slim curved legs
of the dainty Victorian rocker remain
feminine and strong after all these years.
Only faded pink rosebuds
reflect the passage of time.
My love of words grew in that chair.
I curled up in Ethel's lap
as she rocked and read to me.

It was a wedding present to her mother.
She rocked and read to Ethel
then gave it to her to rock her baby,
but he died at birth.
There were no more babies
so Ethel showered her love on me,
her godchild.

Years later, when my belly grew with life,
Ethel gave me her prized possession.
Refinished and reupholstered,
it proudly entered my house
and sat by the waiting crib.
When my baby came,
I rocked and read to her
in that chair.

Now, so many years later
my daughter rocks and reads
to her daughter
in Ethel's rocking chair—
another life nurtured
nestled in the lap of love.

WAITING IN THE WOODS

waiting, alone in a cabin in the woods
dark…silent
Waiting for what?
An image to crash through the door and
thrust itself inside me?
A wild whim to squeeze through a window and
create illusions?
Light to fill the void?
Night sounds invade the silence
a soft rustle, a croak, a buzz,
short breaths, a swallow, a cough, an irregular beat.
A sharp mind.
My persona…a black and white mask,
a divided self, left black, right white.
Remove that mask…my face.
Right side illuminated.
Imagination emerges.
My heart is the drum of life
beating its rhythm
filling me with creation.
Listen to me.
I want out. Can't you hear me?
I writhe in pain
birthing my story.
Metaphors materialize.
My words are music
waiting for a tune.
My thoughts are vessels
wishing for wind.
Visions vibrate, voices pulsate,
silent sounds spiral,
I'm energized.
I burst with exuberance.
My story breathes
cries out in the night
demystifies the darkness.
Alone in a cabin in the woods
spent…at peace.

BUT SHE STAYS

Rage winds
around her colon
grabs her heart
shakes it,
shouts
listen, fool,
run.

But he smiles
desire dances
around her head
clouds her brain
caresses it,
whispers
my love,
stay.

He pulls
rage through
her hungry lips,
teases it, strokes it,
makes promises
she knows are empty.

Again rage shouts
run, run, run
but
she stays.

SCARS

The surgeon entered the O.R. like
a knight in shining white
slit her belly like
a fisherman filets his catch.
Needles, tubes, multicolored fluids
in and out.
Purple scar will fade.

The lover entered her life like
a rainbow after a storm
broke her heart like
ice snaps a branch.
Needles, pills, amber fluids
in and out.
Another purple scar.

SECRETS IN THE SAUCE

When red tomatoes pop,
pluck them, peel them
squeeze them into nectar
and boil till bubbles boogie.
Then dust with yesterday's onions
tears will salt the skeletons
stewing in bouquets of basil.

Simmer the sauce,
stir till senses salivate
swirl into mounds of make-believe
and season with savory secrets.
Then crumble May's red roses
sprinkle into graves of garlic and
cover with sprigs of parsley.

When flavors embrace,
scoop out some sauce,
break some bread,
dip up disappointments,
dip up dreams,
dip up dances.
Dive into the Chianti.
Cha-cha to life's concerto.

THE WAY IT WAS

Near the end of a street overgrown
with debris and potholes
in this budding season of rebirth
an abandoned house sits in the sunshine
like a betrayed lover
left for greener pastures
boarded up windows,
peeling paint once white
empty eyes in a wrinkled face—
If voices of the past could talk
would they tell of
joy that packed up and left or
promises snapped
like ice snaps frozen branches or
just another foreclosed dream?
I wonder about this
abandoned house as I continue down
this zigzagging street—driving over
joy and promises and dreams—
driving into streets
of other abandoned houses
driving away from this once prosperous city
sadly remembering the way it was
hoping the warm Spring rains
will baptize it with new life.

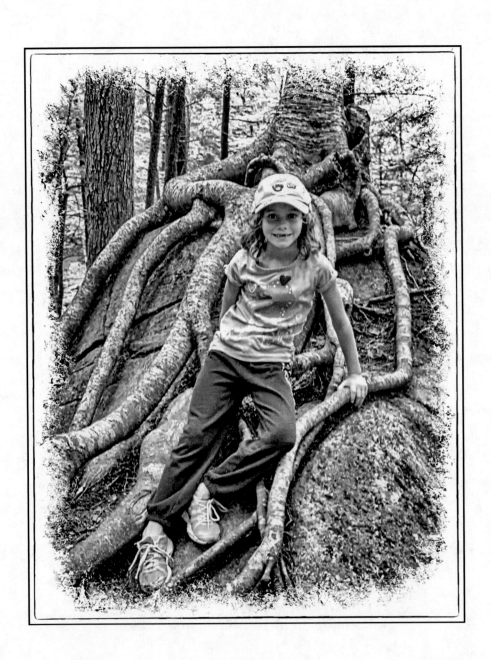

ROOTS

fresh from the womb
newborn babe
inhales independence
cries in celebration

my granddaughter
words so warm they kiss my lips
blood of my ancestors
flows through tiny veins
my past, present in my arms

my daughter—
her daughter at her breast
a gift of grace
a glimpse of heaven
a little hand to hold

daughter's joy
mother's love
grandmother's glee—
rapturous

THE OTHER SIDE OF THE BED

I watched a friend die last week
I watched him flail and gasp for air
and rage for relief—
then that final breath
when the angel of death
released him from his burnt-up lungs.

I watched his wife at the side of his bed
I watched her eyes stare straight ahead
barren as branches in winter—
I wanted to say that sorrow will cease
that spring will green again with peace
but I just sat and watched
from the other side of the bed.

THE BLACK TEACUP

My grandmother's black teacup
shattered on my kitchen floor
    a black teacup
keeps witches away, she said
now I don't have one—
    I pick up the handle and
see her with cup in hand
pinkie out—prayerful
afternoon tea—a solemn ritual.
    Sit up straight, put the napkin
on your lap, don't gulp…
    Her words whispered
in the air as I swept away the past
buried memories in the trash
and wondered about the witches.

WORDS OF HER LIFE

The girl wrote of ritual and religion
of contrition, confession, communion
of unanswered questions, lack of faith
a soul blackened by sin
sinking in a sea of temptation.

The woman wrote of passion and penance
of desire, disappointment, divorce
of dreams shattered like shells
strangled in seaweed, and high hopes
drowned like a spent swimmer.

Now in life's November, she writes
of memories and mortality
of the unknown, the uncertainty
fully alive in the moment, yet
wishing to nail waves to the shore.

ACKNOWLEDGEMENTS

"Words of Her Life," "Unglued," and "Secrets in the Sauce" appeared in **Flutter Poetry Journal** (on-line) January, 2007
"Unglued" appeared in **Upstream 3, A Mohawk Valley Review, 2013.**

"Gray Autumn Mornings" appeared in **The River Reporter's Literary Gazette,** 2008, and in **YOUR DAILY POEM** (on-line) on November 3, 2013.

"Miss Dickinson," "I Wonder," and "Requiem" (Now titled "LEMON MERINGUE PIE AT MIDNIGHT") appeared in **Joyful Poetry** (on-line) May, 2009.

"Over Troubled Water," appeared in **The River Reporter's Literary Gazette, 2009.**

"Far From Home" appeared in **The River Reporter's Literary Gazette,** 2010, and
Upstream 3, A Mohawk Valley Review, 2013.

"The Red Umbrella" appeared in **THE NASSAU COUNTY POET LAUREATE SOCIETY REVIEW,** 2012 and **Upstream 3, A Mohawk Valley Review, 2013.**

"In a Waiting Room" appeared in **Upstream 3, A Mohawk Valley Review,** 2013.

"Where I Come From" appeared in **Upstream 3, A Mohawk Valley Review,** 2013.

"Different Altars" will appear in **THE NASSAU COUNTY POET LAUREATE SOCIETY REVIEW to be published in 2014.**